Table of Contents

Spicy Bacon Cheeseburger

Prep Time: 10 minutes • **Cook Time:** 15 minutes
Makes 4 servings

2	tablespoons **FRANK'S**® **RedHot**® Original Cayenne Pepper Sauce
2	tablespoons barbecue sauce
1	pound lean ground beef
¼	cup FRENCH'S® Worcestershire Sauce
½	teaspoon garlic powder
4	hamburger rolls
4	slices American cheese
4	cooked bacon strips

COMBINE FRANK'S RedHot Original Cayenne Pepper Sauce and barbecue sauce; set aside.

MIX beef, Worcestershire sauce and garlic powder; shape into 4 burgers.

GRILL over medium heat 15 minutes or until cooked through, turning once.

PLACE burgers on rolls. Top *each* with *1* slice of cheese, *1 tablespoon* **FRANK'S RedHot** mixture and *1* piece bacon.

Buffalo-Style Chicken Nachos

Prep Time: 5 minutes • **Cook Time:** 5 minutes
Makes 4 servings

- 2 cups diced, cooked chicken
- ⅓ cup **FRANK'S® RedHot®** Original Cayenne Pepper Sauce
- 2 tablespoons melted butter
- 1 bag (10 ounces) tortilla chips
- 3 cups shredded Cheddar *or* Monterey Jack cheese

PREHEAT oven to 350°F. Combine chicken, **FRANK'S RedHot** Original Cayenne Pepper Sauce and butter. Layer chips, chicken and cheese in ovenproof serving dish or baking dish.

BAKE 5 minutes just until cheese melts. Garnish as desired. Splash on more **FRANK'S RedHot** Original Cayenne Pepper Sauce to taste.

Buffalo Onions

Prep Time: 10 minutes • **Cook Time:** 10 minutes
Makes 6 side-dish servings

½ cup **FRANK'S® RedHot® Original Cayenne Pepper Sauce**
½ cup (1 stick) butter *or* margarine, melted *or* olive oil
¼ cup barbecue sauce
1 tablespoon chili powder (optional)
4 large sweet onions, cut into ½-inch-thick slices

WHISK together **FRANK'S RedHot** Original Cayenne Pepper Sauce, butter, barbecue sauce and chili powder in medium bowl until blended; brush on onion slices.

GRILL onions over medium heat 10 minutes or until tender, turning and brushing frequently with **FRANK'S RedHot** mixture.

TIPS

Onions may be prepared ahead and grilled just before serving.

_____

To make Grilled Buffalo Garlic Bread, combine *¼ cup each* **FRANK'S RedHot** Sauce and melted butter with *1 teaspoon* minced garlic. Lightly brush on thick slices of Italian bread. Grill or toast until golden. Top with blue cheese crumbles, if desired.

FRANK'S® RedHot®
Buffalo Chicken Dip

Prep Time: 5 minutes • **Cook Time:** 20 minutes
Makes 3½ cups dip

- **1** package (8 ounces) PHILADELPHIA® Cream Cheese, softened
- **½** cup any flavor **FRANK'S® RedHot® Original Cayenne Pepper Sauce** *or* **FRANK'S® RedHot® Buffalo Wings Sauce**
- **½** cup blue cheese *or* ranch dressing
- **½** cup crumbled blue cheese *or* your favorite shredded cheese
- **2** cups shredded cooked chicken

PREHEAT oven to 350°F.

COMBINE all ingredients in 1-quart baking dish.

BAKE 20 minutes or until mixture is heated through; stir.

Microwave Directions: Prepare as above. Place in microwave-safe dish. Microwave, uncovered, on HIGH 5 minutes until hot, stirring halfway through cooking.

Slow Cooker Method: Prepare as above. Place mixture in 1½-quart slow cooker. Cover and cook on High 1½ hours or Low 2½ hours or until hot.

Tailgating Tip: Prepare dip ahead and place in heavy disposable foil pan. Place pan on grill and heat dip until hot and bubbly.

TIP
Substitute 2 (10-ounce) cans white premium chunk chicken breast in water, drained, for cooked chicken.

Tailgate Wing Sampler

Prep Time: 10 minutes • **Cook Time:** 30 minutes
Makes 6 servings

2½	pounds chicken wings
½	cup **FRANK'S® RedHot® Original Cayenne Pepper Sauce**
⅓	cup butter *or* margarine, melted
	Blue cheese dressing
	Celery sticks

CUT off wing tips from chicken wings; discard. Cut wings in half between remaining joint to make two pieces. Grill over medium heat 30 minutes or until thoroughly cooked and crispy, turning often. Place in large bowl.

COMBINE FRANK'S RedHot Original Cayenne Pepper Sauce and butter. Pour over wings; toss well to coat evenly. Serve wings with blue cheese dressing and celery sticks.

Shanghai Red Wings: Cook wings as directed. Combine ¼ *cup* soy sauce, *3 tablespoons* **FRANK'S RedHot** Sauce, *3 tablespoons* honey, *2 tablespoons* peanut oil, *1 teaspoon* grated peeled fresh ginger and *1 teaspoon* minced garlic in small bowl; mix well. Pour over wings; toss well to coat evenly.

Cajun Wings: Cook wings as directed. Combine ⅓ *cup* **FRANK'S RedHot** Sauce, *⅓ cup* ketchup, *¼ cup (½ stick)* melted butter or margarine and *2 teaspoons* Cajun seasoning blend in small bowl; mix well. Pour over wings; toss well to coat evenly.

Santa Fe Wings: Cook wings as directed. Combine ¼ *cup* **FRANK'S RedHot** Sauce, *¼ cup (½ stick)* melted butter or margarine, *¼ cup* chili sauce and *1 teaspoon* chili powder in small bowl; mix well. Pour over wings; toss well to coat evenly.

Spicy Fish Tacos with Fresh Salsa

Prep Time: 15 minutes • **Marinate Time:** 30 minutes • **Cook Time:** 5 minutes
Makes 4 to 6 servings

- ¾ cup plus 2 tablespoons **FRANK'S® RedHot®** Original Cayenne Pepper Sauce, divided
- 1 pound thick, firm white fish fillets, such as cod, halibut *or* sea bass, cut into ¾-inch cubes
- ½ cup sour cream
- 1½ cups finely chopped plum tomatoes
- ¼ cup minced cilantro
- 2 tablespoons minced red onion
- 8 taco shells, warmed
- 2 cups shredded lettuce

POUR *½ cup* **FRANK'S RedHot** Original Cayenne Pepper Sauce over fish in resealable food storage plastic bag or bowl. Marinate in refrigerator 30 minutes.

COMBINE *¼ cup* **FRANK'S RedHot** Original Cayenne Pepper Sauce and sour cream in small bowl; chill until needed.

COMBINE tomatoes, cilantro, onion and remaining *2 tablespoons* **FRANK'S RedHot** Original Cayenne Pepper Sauce. Reserve.

REMOVE fish from marinade. Spray large nonstick skillet with nonstick cooking spray and heat over medium heat until hot. Stir-fry fish 3 to 5 minutes until just opaque and flakes with fork. Fill each taco shell with shredded lettuce, cooked fish and salsa. Drizzle with sour cream mixture.

Variation: Substitute *1 pound* peeled and deveined shrimp for fish.

Shrimp on the Barbie

Prep Time: 10 minutes • **Cook Time:** 10 minutes
Makes 4 servings

1   pound large raw shrimp, shelled and deveined
1   *each* red and yellow bell pepper, seeded and cut into 1-inch chunks
4   slices lime (optional)
½   cup prepared smoky-flavor barbecue sauce
2   tablespoons FRENCH'S® Worcestershire Sauce
2   tablespoons **FRANK'S**® **RedHot**® Original Cayenne Pepper Sauce
1   clove garlic, minced

THREAD shrimp, peppers and lime, if desired, alternately onto metal skewers. Combine barbecue sauce, Worcestershire, **FRANK'S RedHot** Original Cayenne Pepper Sauce and garlic in small bowl; mix well.

GRILL kabobs over high heat 10 minutes or until shrimp turn pink, turning and basting often with sauce mixture. Serve warm.

Buffalo Chicken Pizza

Prep Time: 15 minutes • **Cook Time:** 15 minutes
Makes 8 servings

2	(12-inch) pre-baked pizza crust shells
1	cup pizza sauce *or* barbecue sauce
½	cup thinly sliced celery
3	cups cooked, diced chicken
½	cup **FRANK'S® RedHot®** Buffalo Wings Sauce
2	cups shredded mozzarella cheese
⅔	cup gorgonzola *or* blue cheese, crumbled

PREHEAT oven to 450°F. Place pizza shells on baking pans. Spread shells with pizza sauce and sprinkle with celery.

TOSS chicken with **FRANK'S RedHot** Buffalo Wings Sauce. Arrange on top of pizzas and top with cheeses.

BAKE pizzas 15 minutes until crust is crispy and cheese melts. Cut into wedges or squares to serve.

Grill Method: Prepare pizzas as above. Place directly on grill rack. Grill over medium heat until cheese melts and pizza crust is crispy.

TIP
You may substitute *6 tablespoons* **FRANK'S RedHot** Original Cayenne Pepper Sauce mixed with *2 tablespoons* melted butter for the Buffalo Wings Sauce.

Chicken Kabobs with Thai Dipping Sauce

Prep Time: 15 minutes • **Cook Time:** 10 minutes
Makes 6 appetizer servings

- 1 pound boneless, skinless chicken breasts, cut into 1-inch cubes
- 1 small cucumber, halved, seeded and cut into thick slices
- 1 cup cherry tomatoes
- 2 green onions, cut into 1-inch pieces
- ⅔ cup teriyaki baste and glaze sauce
- ⅓ cup **FRANK'S® RedHot®** Original Cayenne Pepper Sauce
- ⅓ cup peanut butter
- 3 tablespoons frozen orange juice concentrate, undiluted
- 2 cloves garlic, minced

THREAD chicken, cucumber, tomatoes and onions alternately onto metal skewers; set aside.

COMBINE teriyaki baste and glaze sauce, **FRANK'S RedHot** Original Cayenne Pepper Sauce, peanut butter, orange juice concentrate and garlic; mix well. Reserve ⅔ *cup* sauce for dipping.

BRUSH skewers with some of remaining sauce. Grill over medium-high heat 10 minutes or until chicken is no longer pink in center, turning and basting often with remaining sauce. Serve skewers with reserved Thai Dipping Sauce.

Texas Smoked BBQ Brisket

Prep Time: 15 minutes • **Marinate Time:** 1 hour • **Cook Time:** 7 hours
Makes 10 to 12 servings

- ½   cup prepared barbecue seasoning
- 2   tablespoons ground chili powder
- 1   (5- to 7-pound) beef brisket, trimmed with a layer of fat (center flat portion)
- 1   cup **FRANK'S® RedHot®** Original Cayenne Pepper Sauce
- 1½   cups beer *or* non-alcoholic malt beverage, divided
- 1   cup **CATTLEMEN'S®** Authentic Smoke House Barbecue Sauce *or* **CATTLEMEN'S®** Award Winning Classic Barbecue Sauce
- ¼   cup (½ stick) butter

COMBINE barbecue seasoning and chili powder. Rub mixture thoroughly into beef. Place meat, fat-side up, into disposable foil pan. Cover and refrigerate 1 to 3 hours. Just before using, prepare mop sauce by combining **FRANK'S RedHot** Original Cayenne Pepper Sauce and *1 cup* beer; set aside.

PREPARE grill for indirect cooking over medium-low heat (250°F). If desired, toss soaked wood chips over coals or heat source. Place pan with meat in center of grill over indirect heat. Cover grill. Cook meat over low heat 6 to 7 hours until meat is very tender (190°F internal temperature). Baste with mop sauce once an hour.

COMBINE barbecue sauce, butter and remaining *½ cup* beer. Simmer 5 minutes until slightly thickened. Slice meat and serve with sauce.

To easily slice meat, cut against the grain using an electric knife.

Spicy BBQ Chicken Pizza

Prep Time: 15 minutes • **Cook Time:** 10 minutes
Makes 8 servings

- 2 cups shredded, cooked chicken (about 1 pound uncooked)
- ¼ cup **FRANK'S® RedHot®** Buffalo Wings Sauce
- 1 pound prepared pizza *or* bread dough (thawed, if frozen)
- 1 cup **CATTLEMEN'S®** Award Winning Classic Barbecue Sauce
- 2 ripe plum tomatoes, diced
- ½ cup finely diced red onion
- ½ cup sliced black olives (2.25-ounce can)
- 2 cups shredded taco blend cheese
  Cilantro *or* green onions, minced (optional)

TOSS chicken with **FRANK'S RedHot** Buffalo Wings Sauce; set aside. Divide dough in half. Gently stretch or roll each piece of dough into 13×9-inch rectangle on floured surface. Coat one side with nonstick cooking spray.

COOK dough, coated side down, on greased grill over medium-high heat for 5 minutes until browned and crisp on bottom. Using tongs, turn dough over. Spread each pizza crust with barbecue sauce and top with chicken mixture, tomatoes, onion, olives and cheese, dividing evenly.

GRILL pizzas about 5 minutes longer until bottom is browned, crispy and cheese melts. Garnish with minced cilantro or green onions, if desired.

Variation: Top pizza with different shredded cheeses, such as Cheddar or Jack, or with other vegetables, such as whole kernel corn, jalapeño or bell peppers.

TIP
For easier handling, allow pizza dough to rest 30 minutes in an oiled, covered bowl at room temperature.

Fireball Vegetarian Chili

Prep Time: 15 minutes • **Cook Time:** 25 minutes
Makes 6 servings

1	tablespoon vegetable oil
1	onion, chopped
2	cloves garlic, minced
2	cans (15 to 19 ounces *each*) red kidney beans, rinsed and drained
1½	cups *each* coarsely chopped zucchini and carrots
1	can (15 ounces) crushed tomatoes in purée, undrained
1	can (7 ounces) whole kernel corn, drained
1	can (4½ ounces) chopped green chilies, drained
¼	cup **FRANK'S® RedHot®** Original Cayenne Pepper Sauce
1	tablespoon ground cumin
	Hot cooked rice
	Sour cream *or* shredded cheese

HEAT oil in large saucepot. Add onion and garlic and cook, stirring occasionally 3 minutes or just until tender. Stir in remaining ingredients except rice, sour cream and cheese.

HEAT to boiling. Reduce heat to medium-low. Cook, partially covered, 20 minutes or until vegetables are tender and flavors are blended. Serve with hot cooked rice. Garnish with sour cream or shredded cheese, if desired.

You can also serve chili over hot baked potatoes.

Easy Buffalo Chicken Mac n' Cheese

Prep Time: 5 minutes • **Cook Time:** 10 minutes
Makes 4 to 6 servings

- 2 boxes (7.25 ounces *each*) macaroni and cheese dinner
- ¾ cup milk
- ½ cup (1 stick) butter
- 2 cups cut-up cooked chicken
- ¼ to ⅓ cup **FRANK'S® RedHot®** Buffalo Wings Sauce *or* **FRANK'S® RedHot®** Original Cayenne Pepper Sauce

PREPARE macaroni and cheese dinner according to package directions, using milk and butter.

STIR in chicken and **FRANK'S RedHot** Sauce. Heat through.

SPOON into serving dish.

FRANK'S® Sweet Chili Cream Cheese Dip

Prep Time: 5 minutes
Makes 10 servings, 2 tablespoons each

1   package (8 ounces) **PHILADELPHIA**® Cream Cheese
1   cup **FRANK'S**® **RedHot**® Sweet Chili Sauce

PLACE cream cheese on serving dish.

POUR FRANK'S RedHot Sweet Chili Sauce evenly over cream cheese.

SERVE with crackers, chips or vegetables.

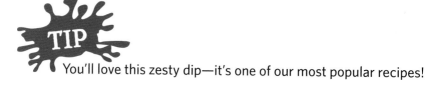

TIP You'll love this zesty dip—it's one of our most popular recipes!